D1223785

VELOCIRAPTOR

by Harold T. Rober

BUMBA BOOKS™

LERNER PUBLICATIONS ◆ MINNEAPOLIS

Note to Educators:

Throughout this book, you'll find critical thinking questions. These can be used to engage young readers in thinking critically about the topic and in using the text and photos to do so.

Lerner Publications Company
A division of Lerner Publishing Group, Inc.
241 First Avenue North
Minneapolis, MN 55401 USA

For reading levels and more information, look up this title at www.lernerbooks.com.

Library of Congress Cataloging-in-Publication Data

Names: Rober, Harold T.
Title: Velociraptor / by Harold T. Rober.
Description: Minneapolis : Lerner Publications, [2017] | Series: Bumba books. Dinosaurs and prehistoric beasts |
    Audience: Age 4–8. | Audience: K to Grade 3. | Includes bibliographical references and index.
Identifiers: LCCN 2016018688 (print) | LCCN 2016023328 (ebook) | ISBN 9781512426410 (lb : alk. paper) |
    ISBN 9781512429176 (pb : alk. paper) | ISBN 9781512427356 (eb pdf)
Subjects: LCSH: Velociraptor—Juvenile literature. | Dinosaurs—Juvenile literature.
Classification: LCC QE862.S3 R5544 2017 (print) | LCC QE862.S3 (ebook) | DDC 567.912—dc23

LC record available at https://lccn.loc.gov/2016018688

Manufactured in the United States of America
1 – VP – 12/31/16

Expand learning beyond the printed book. Download free, complementary educational resources for this book from our website, www.lerneresource.com.

Table of Contents

Velociraptor Ran

Velociraptor was a kind

of dinosaur.

It lived millions

of years ago.

It is extinct.

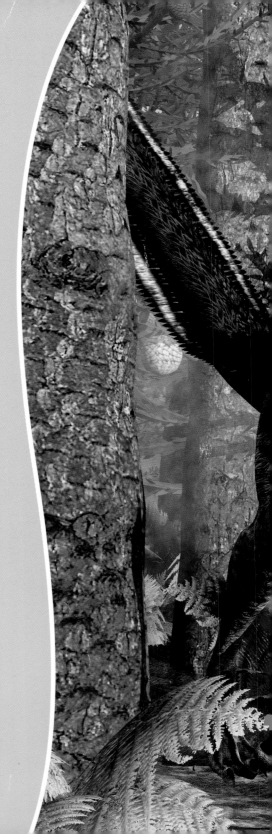

Velociraptor was small.

It was the size of a turkey.

Velociraptor was fast.

It ran on two legs.

It chased smaller animals.

Why do you think velociraptor chased smaller animals?

Each foot had a sharp claw.

Velociraptor used these claws

to hold down prey.

Sharp teeth filled

velociraptor's mouth.

These teeth bit into prey.

Velociraptor had a long tail.

The tail helped

velociraptor balance.

Velociraptor had feathers.

But it could not fly.

Its arms were too short.

**Why would
short arms
make it hard
to fly?**

Feathers may have
helped velociraptor
stay warm.

They may have helped
velociraptor run faster.

Velociraptors built nests.

They laid eggs there.

What other animals make nests and lay eggs?

Parts of a Velociraptor

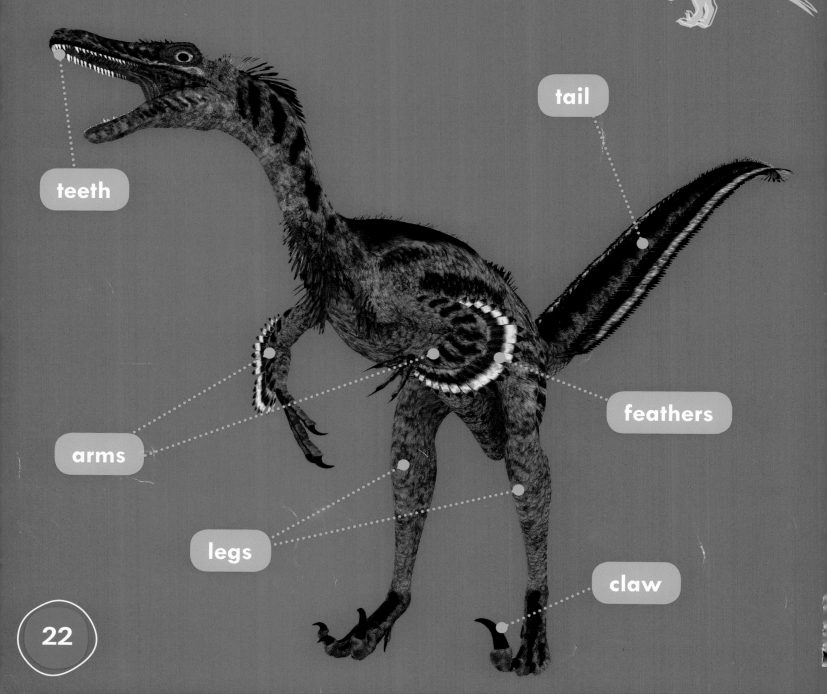

teeth

tail

feathers

arms

legs

claw

Picture Glossary

balance

to keep steady and upright

claw

a hard, sharp nail

extinct

no longer alive

prey

an animal that is hunted by another animal

23

Index

Read More

Gray, Susan H. *Velociraptor.* Mankato, MN: Child's World, 2015.

Rober, Harold T. *Pterodactyl.* Minneapolis: Lerner Publications, 2017.

Silverman, Buffy. *Can You Tell a Velociraptor from a Deinonychus?* Minneapolis: Lerner Publications, 2014.

Photo Credits